S0-APM-948

BEYOND BEDSIDE MANNER

99 Ways
To Show You Care

K.C. Warner, R.Ph.

Beyond Bedside Manner:
99 Ways to Show You Care.
K.C. Warner, R.Ph.
American Media Incorporated

Editor: Shari Cannon
Design: Mervil Paylor Design

All rights reserved. No part of this book may be reproduced or transmitted in any form or by any means now known or to be invented, electronic or mechanical, including photocopying, recording, or by any information storage or retrieval system without written permission from the author or publisher, except for the brief inclusion of quotations in a review.

Copyright©1997, Warner Development
Printed in the United States of America

Warner Development books may be obtained by contacting Warner Development, PO Box 470317, Charlotte, NC 28247-0317, telephone 704.845.6108, facsimile: 704.845.2693 or American Media Incorporated, 4900 University Avenue, West Des Moines, IA 50266-6769 telephone 800.262.2557, facsimile: 515.224.0256.

Library of Congress catalog card number 97-074355
Warner Development
Beyond Bedside Manner: 99 Ways to Show You Care.
ISBN 1-884926-81-9

This book is dedicated in loving memory to my husband's mother and my special friend, Theresa Warner, a nurse who continually demonstrated her commitment to patient and family care. In addition, this book is dedicated to Hospice, who, together with Theresa, taught me more about patient care than I could ever begin to describe in print. Thank you.

Sincere appreciation is extended to those who contributed to the ideas in this book:

Shari Cannon, Blackwell Regional Hospital

Laura K. Davis, Davis Designs

Dan Raymond, PPI

Paula Snyder, St. Vincent's Healthcare System

Michael Scott, Empowerment Unlimited

Michael Williams, GlaxoWellcome

Be positive.

*Our thoughts dictate
the outcome of our lives.*

1

Celebrate health.

Health is a tremendous accomplishment. Enjoy it!

Sharpen up.

*Patient-satisfaction skills
are acquired skills.*

Live well.

Wellness is a state of being.

4

Discover your uniqueness.

Our differences make us beautiful.

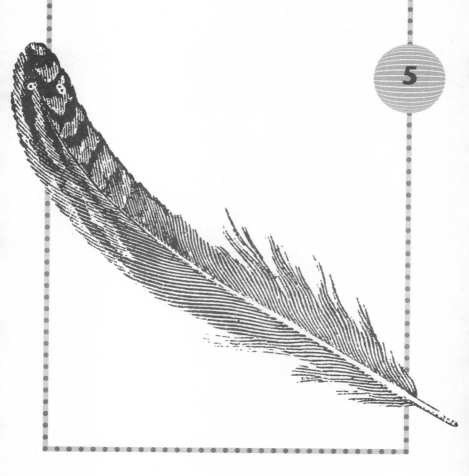

5

Look
for humor.

Laughter is amazing medicine.

Focus on what's important.

*Our focus
determines our future.*

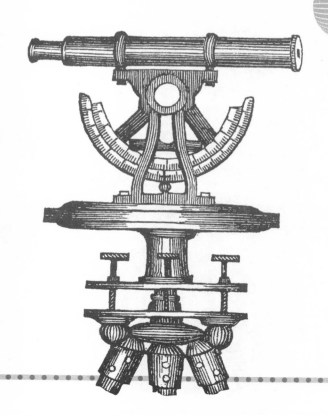

Be prepared.

Preparation produces powerful results.

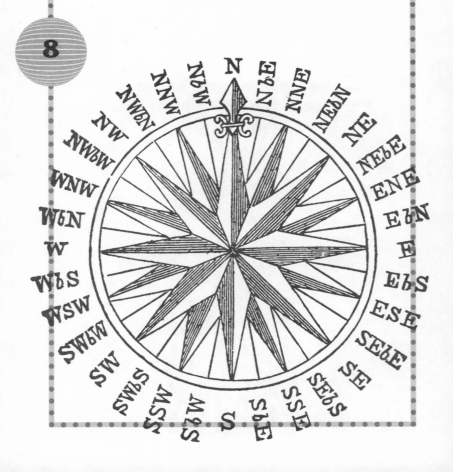

Be flexible.

*New ideas emerge
when we consider new ways
to approach old habits.*

9

Be grateful.

Appreciation impacts care.

Expect
the best.

You will get it.

11

Believe.

Miracles are the direct result of unwavering belief.

12

Serve.

*When we serve,
we receive the bounty.*

13

Give.

*Our time, our talents
make a difference.*

14

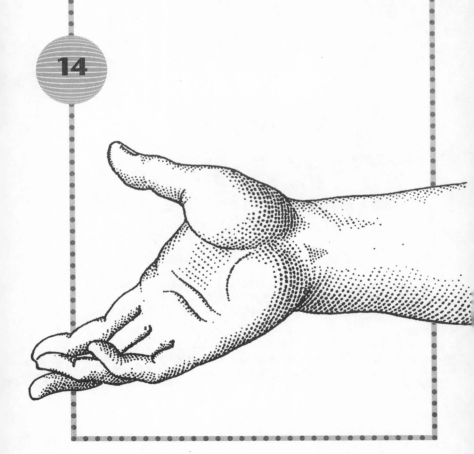

Ask.

*What can we do
to make you better?*

15

Listen.

*Respect our patient's opinion
and self-diagnosis.*

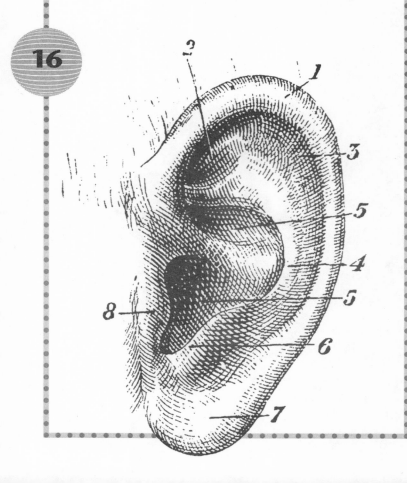

Believe.

*Others sense what we believe
to be true.*

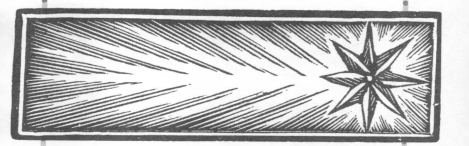

Reconsider.

*How many ways are there
to solve a problem?*

Make it easy.

Some processes are simply easy.
Keep them that way.

19

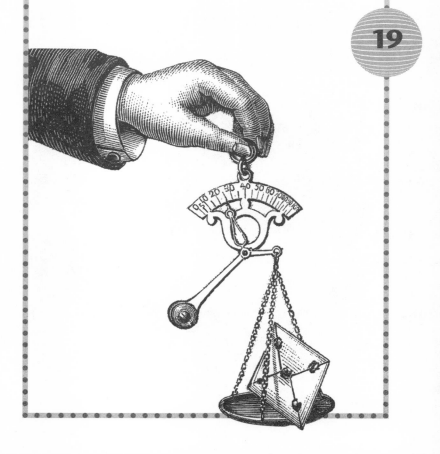

Do a great job.

What self-satisfaction we know when we say to ourselves, "well done."

20

Diagnose.

*Dig deep to
uncover the answer.*

Maximize your style.

Only you can be you.
Do it well.

22

Treat the family.

The entire family influences illness and wellness.

Discover it within.

*Our power, our mastery
is discovered.*

Think it through.

*Picture your success
and how you will achieve it.*

25

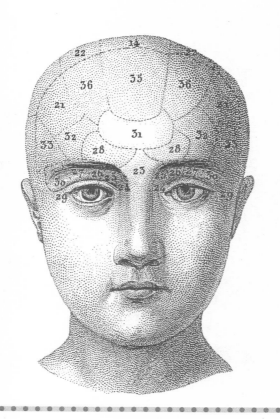

Notice your belief system.

What do you believe?
Stay true.

It's about the belief.

Believe that you can make a difference.

Be true to yourself.

You are the only one who can determine your level of performance.

28

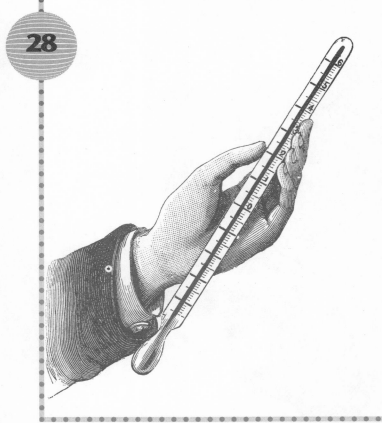

Be your best every time.

Brave souls conquer.

29

Give.

Think of how you feel when you give time and energy to your patients.

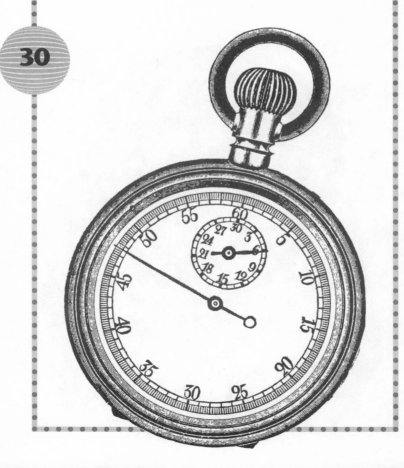

Smile.

*Sometimes a caring smile
is all it takes.*

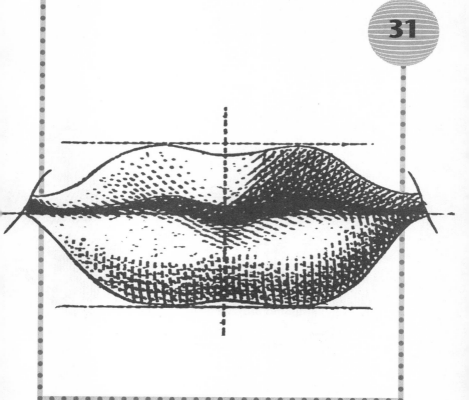

Make connections.

*Others contribute
to our success, too.*

32

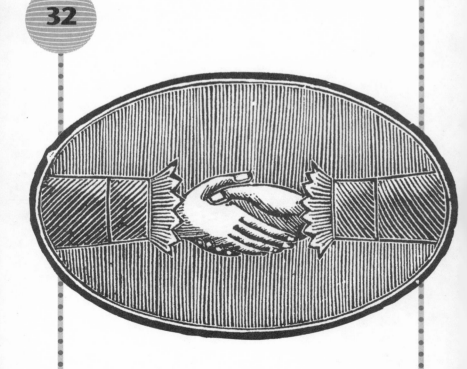

Make a difference.

We all can.

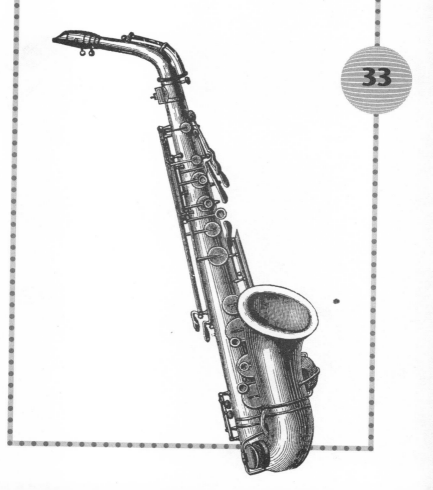

Search.

*What else can we
do to solve the problem?*

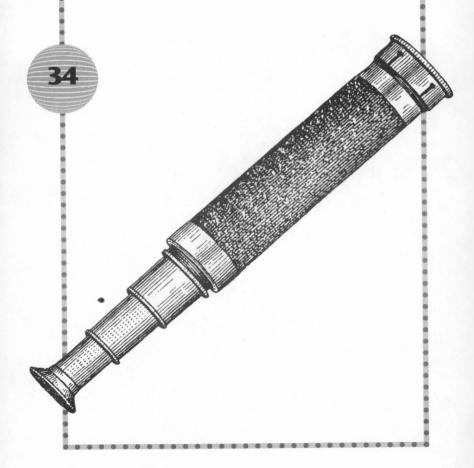

Administer powerful medicine.

Our most powerful medicine is demonstrating respect and concern.

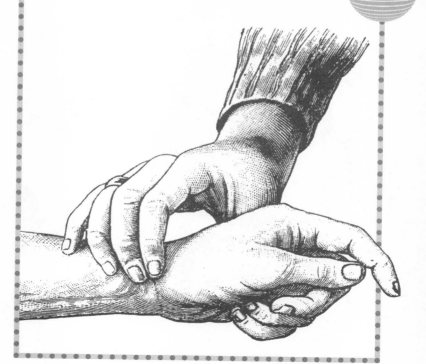

Learn.

Our potential to learn surpasses
all imagination.

Care for health.

*Do you remember
why you chose healthcare
in the beginning?*

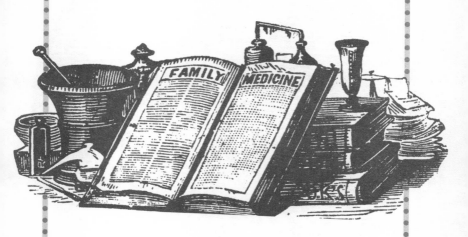

Maximize
relationships.

Relationships drive success.

38

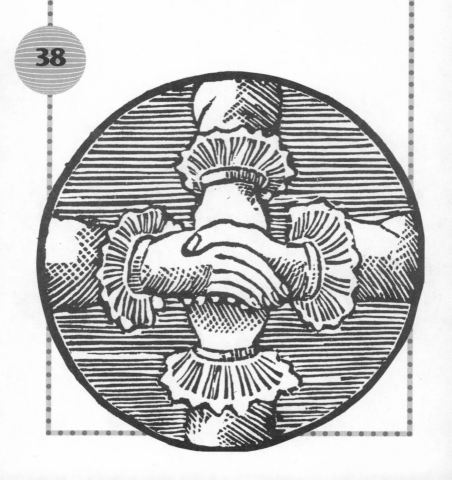

Connect.

Look deep into another soul.

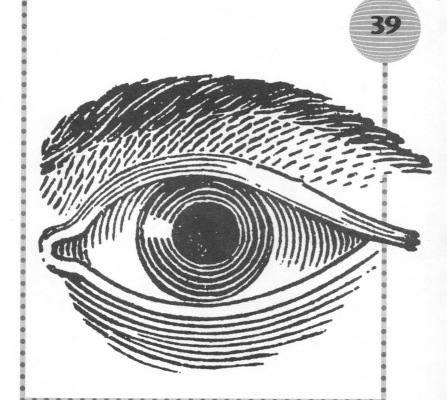

Organize your thoughts.

Our thoughts drive our actions and, thus, our future.

40

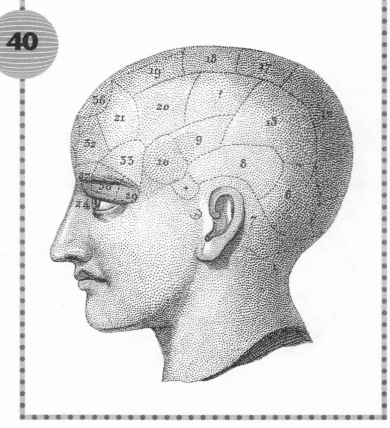

Watch your wellness.

*Am I a model
for my patient's behavior?*

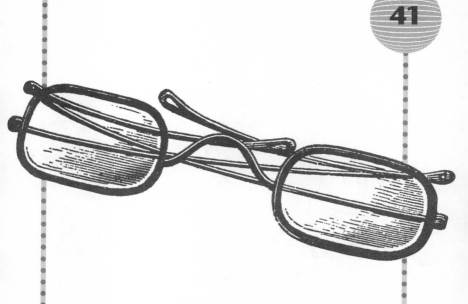

Motivate.

There is great potential in others and ourselves.

Plan.

Prepare for greatness.

43

Check outcomes.

*Do we see the
fruits of our labor?*

Pat on the back.

It feels great.
Remember to do it.

45

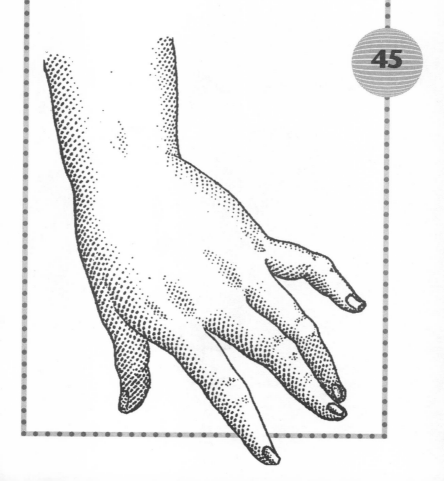

Appreciate.

Appreciate health, nature, others.
What else?

46

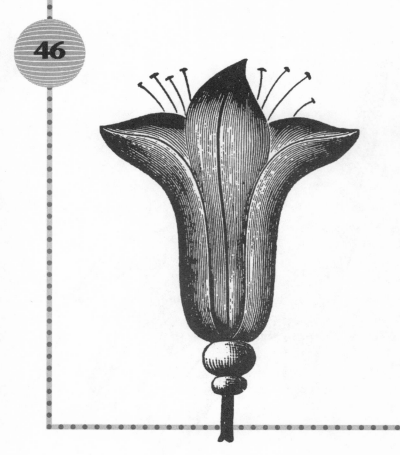

Touch.

Human contact connects.

Congratulate.

Success should be shared.

48

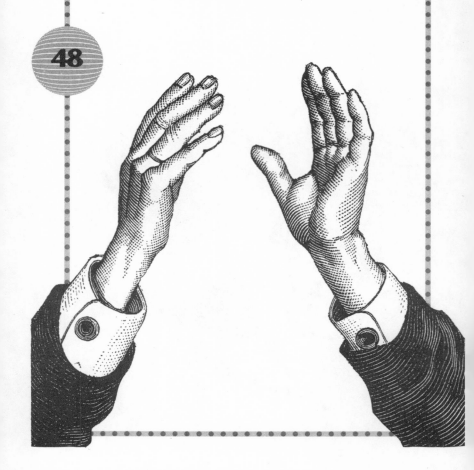

Write it out.

Plans are much less intimidating on paper.

49

Apply
your best.

Give it your best —
only your best.

Create the future.

Our future depends upon our actions today.

51

Respond.

*Decide to make
a difference.*

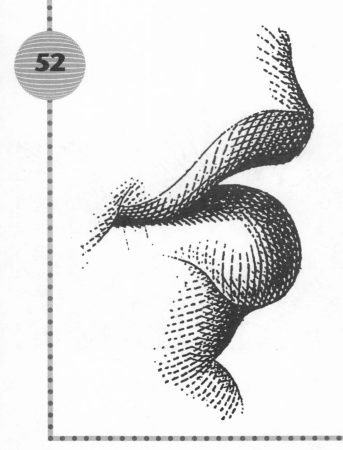

Look them in the eye.

Patients appreciate honesty.

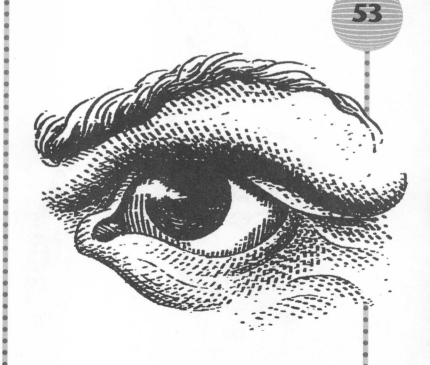

Big hug.

*Sometimes that is
all it takes.*

Inspire others.

Others inspire us, too.

Recognize excellence.

Excellence needs to be acknowledged.

56

Search to understand.

Where is the meaning?

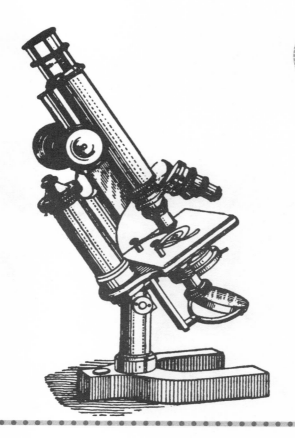

Plan for wellness.

*Look for possibilities
to become better.*

Negotiate for health.

*What can we do
to be healthy today?*

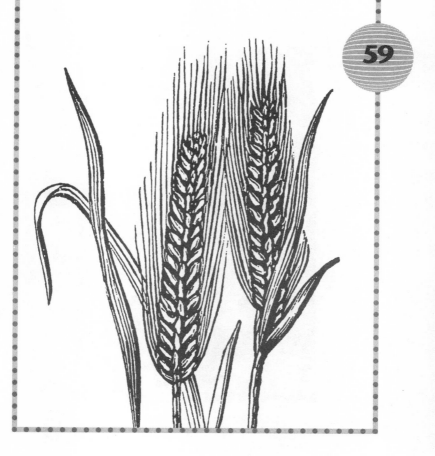

Set the example.

Inspire great work.

Aim for achievement.

We can do it!

61

Praise
health.

*Isn't it wonderful
when we feel healthy?*

Appreciate teamwork.

And team members.

Orchestrate learning.

Learning requires preparation and awareness.

Seek
harmony.

*We achieve much more when
we are pulling together.*

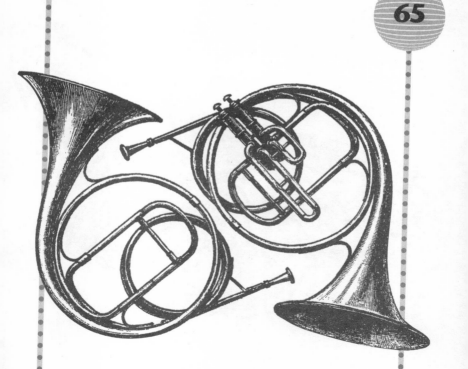

Grasp change.

It moves us forward.

Challenge.

*It takes courage to stand up
for what is right.*

67

Demonstrate confidence.

*Others will accept
our approach.*

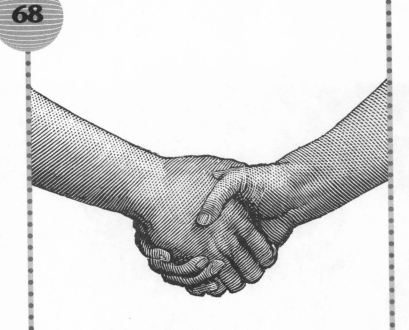

Influence
greatness.

Our part is significant.

Look for greatness.

It is everywhere,
in everyone.

Dream.

*When sleeping
and when awake.*

Encourage care.

Caring involves the entire healthcare team.

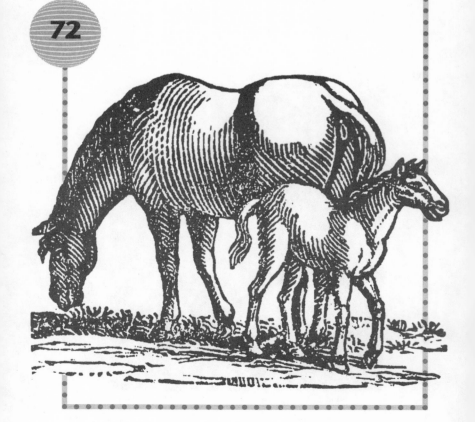

Picture perfection.

What would it look like to provide optimum care?

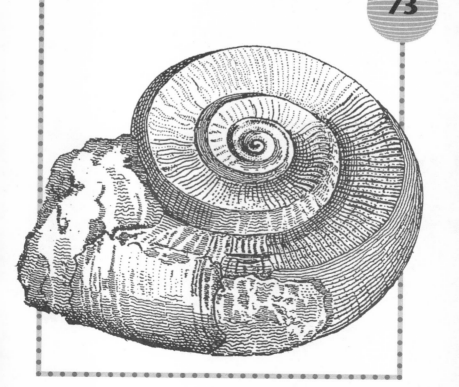

Invent
options.

What is possible?

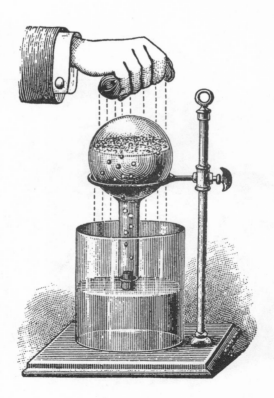

Demonstrate empathy.

We care.
Now let's show it to those
who need it the most.

Agree.

Find common ground
and move forward from there.

76

Share
emotions.

Emotions show we are human.
Embrace them.

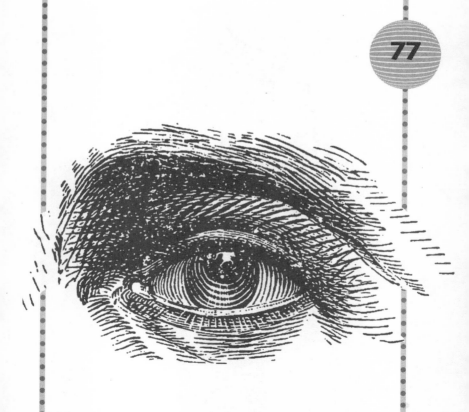

Model.

Show others what it looks like to be brilliant.

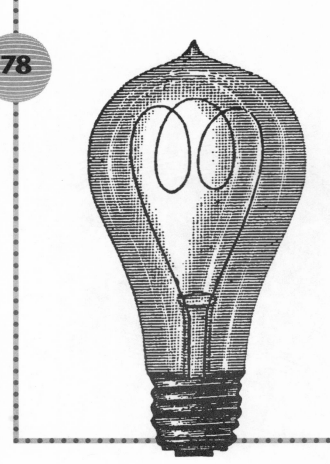

Call to check up.

Major impact!

79

Build a strong foundation.

Know our base, our core.

80

Keep
in touch.

Show you care.

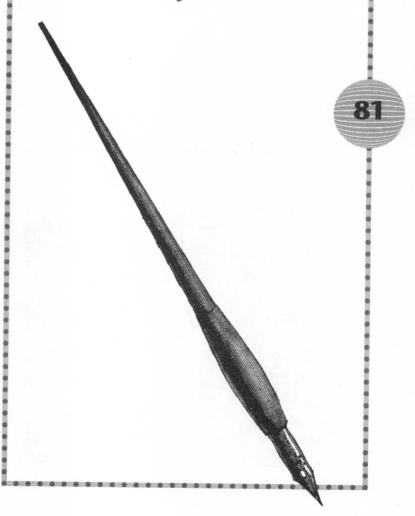

Empower.

*Others can achieve
great things, too.
Let them.*

Laugh.

It feels good.

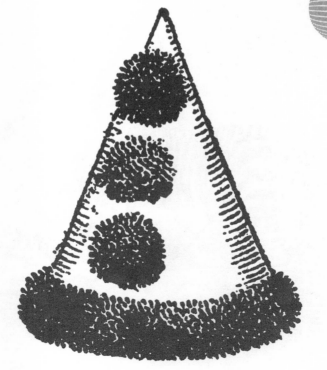

Study the unusual.

What can we learn?

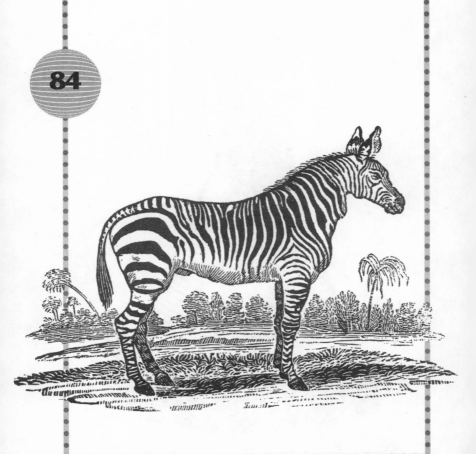

Express concern.

Show you care.

Keep confidences.

Be careful when comparing.
"You are the fifth flu
I have seen today."

Display credibility.

Patients determine their quality of care by the communication skills of the clinician.

87

Donate.

Doesn't it feel great?

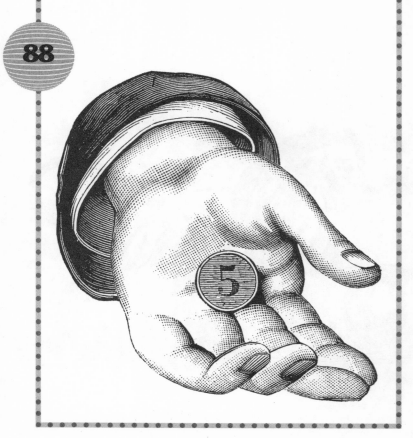

Become a pioneer.

Enhance and embrace change.

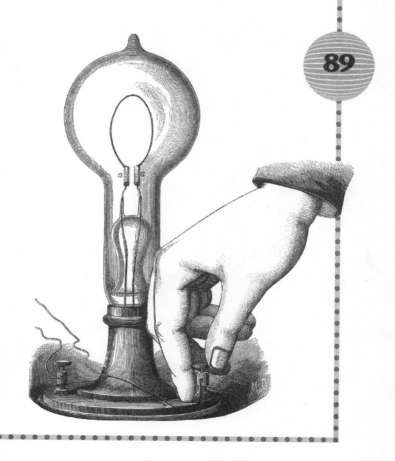

89

Crush fear.

Fear has no place in creating a powerful future.

90

Notice
the family.

*The family
inspires wellness.*

91

Become thrilled.

Our emotions paint the day.

Unite purposes.

Find someone who shares your dream.

Exemplify care.

Caring is contagious.

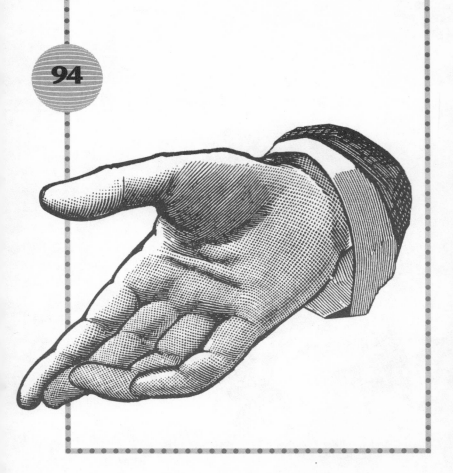

Love.

What else is there?

Expand your knowledge.

*Learning is
essential to growing.*

Manage excellence.

*Others demonstrate
excellence, too.*

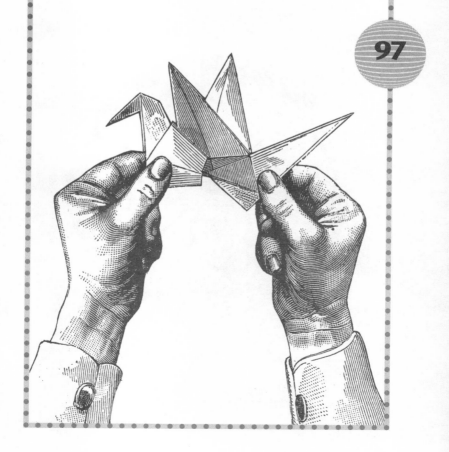

Invest in your development.

We can become better and better at what we do.

98

Invite responsibility.

Take it.
You will do a super job.

99